The Outcome of the American Revolution

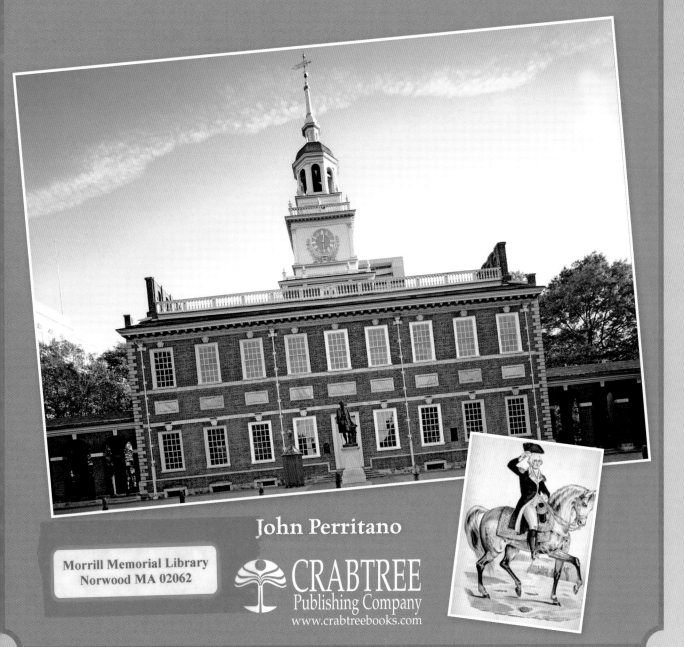

John Perritano

CRABTREE
Publishing Company
www.crabtreebooks.com

Understanding
The American Revolution

J973.4
Perritano

30.60

Author: John Perritano
Publishing plan research and development:
Sean Charlebois, Reagan Miller
Crabtree Publishing Company
Editors: Leslie Jenkins, Janet Sweet, Kirsten Holm, Lynn Peppas
Proofreaders: Lisa Slone, Kelly McNiven
Editorial director: Kathy Middleton
Production coordinator: Shivi Sharma
Creative director: Amir Abbasi
Cover design: Samara Parent, Margaret Amy Salter
Photo research: Nivisha Sinha
Maps: Paul Brinkdopke
Production coordinator and prepress technician: Samara Parent
Print coordinator: Katherine Berti

Written, developed, and produced by Planman Technologies

Cover: A painting by John Trumbull shows British officer Lord Cornwallis surrendering at Yorktown, ending the war.
Title page: (Main) Both the Declaration of Independence and the United States Constitution were debated and adopted at Independence Hall in Philadelphia.
(bottom) A painting portrays George Washington riding to his inauguration as president.

Photographs and Reproductions
Front Cover: Wikimedia Commons / Architect of the Capitol (b), Shutterstock (t); Title Page: Library of Congress; Library of Congress; Table of Content: ©Visions of America, LLC / Alamy / IndiaPicture; Architect of the Capitol; ©Stock Montage, Inc. / Alamy / IndiaPicture; Library of Congress; Library of Congress; Library of Congress; Introduction: Library of Congress; Chapter 1: Library of Congress; Chapter 2: Library of Congress; Chapter 3: Library of Congress; Chapter 4: Library of Congress; Chapter 5: Library of Congress; Page 4: ©Visions of America, LLC / Alamy / IndiaPicture; Page 5: Library of Congress; Page 8: Architect of the Capitol; Page 9: ©INTERFOTO / Alamy / IndiaPicture; Page 14: Library of Congress; Page 15: Library of Congress; Page 16: Library of Congress; Page 17: Library of Congress; Page 18: Library of Congress; Page 20: Library of Congress; Page 21: ©Stock Montage, Inc. / Alamy / IndiaPicture; Page 23: larry1235 / Shutterstock; Page 25: ©PRISMA ARCHIVO / Alamy / IndiaPicture; Page 27: Library of Congress; Page 28: Library of Congress; Page 29: Library of Congress; Page 30: Library of Congress; Page 32: CREATISTA / Shutterstock.com; Page 33: Shutterstock; Page 34: Library of Congress; Page 35: ©PARIS PIERCE / Alamy / IndiaPicture; Page 37: Library of Congress; Page 38: Library of Congress; Page 39: Library of Congress; Page 41: Library of Congress; (t = top, b = bottom, l = left, c = center, r = right, bkgd = background, fgd = foreground)

Library and Archives Canada Cataloguing in Publication

Perritano, John
          The outcome of the American Revolution / John Perritano.

(Understanding the American Revolution)
Includes index.
Issued also in electronic format.
ISBN 978-0-7787-0805-6 (bound).--ISBN 978-0-7787-0816-2 (pbk.)

          1. United States--Politics and government--1783-1809--Juvenile literature. 2. United States--History--Revolution, 1775-1783-- Influence--Juvenile literature. I. Title. II. Series: Understanding the American Revolution (St. Catharines, Ont.)

E303.P47 2013   j973.4   C2013-900228-6

Library of Congress Cataloging-in-Publication Data

CIP available at Library of Congress

Crabtree Publishing Company

www.crabtreebooks.com   1-800-387-7650

Printed in Canada/022013/BF20130114

Published in Canada
Crabtree Publishing
616 Welland Ave.
St. Catharines, Ontario
L2M 5V6

Published in the United States
Crabtree Publishing
PMB 59051
350 Fifth Avenue, 59th Floor
New York, New York 10118

Published in the United Kingdom
Crabtree Publishing
Maritime House
Basin Road North, Hove
BN41 1WR

Published in Australia
Crabtree Publishing
3 Charles Street
Coburg North
VIC 3058

TABLE *of* CONTENTS

Introduction
Rising Sun

4

Freedom Around the Corner
Surrender at Yorktown | Peace Talks | A New Government |
Land Grab | The Call Goes Out | What to Do?

1

8

A New Constitution
On to Philadelphia | Debate Begins |
The Great Compromise | The Issue of Slavery

2

16

The Great Debate
To the States | Selling the Constitution | Opposition |
Hancock, Once Again | America's Bill of Rights

3

26

Governing in a Free Land
The Nation's Father | What to Do? |
Establishing a Court System | Party Time |
The Nation's Money

4

34

The American Legacy
A Worldwide Impact

5

40

Glossary, 42 | Timeline, 44 | Further Reading and Websites, 45 | Bibliography, 46 | Index, 47

Introduction

T he Revolutionary War had ended. George Washington was tired and longed to go home to Mount Vernon, his sprawling Virginia estate. But he still had work to do. He had helped create a nation. Now it was time to preserve it.

Major Events

1775
April
Revolutionary War begins

1781
October 19
British **surrender** at Yorktown

1783
September 3
Treaty of Paris signed

Rising Sun

When Washington took charge of the Continental Army in 1775, America was made up of 13 unhappy British colonies. Yet, the colonies achieved the unthinkable by freeing themselves from the greatest world power of the age—Great Britain.

George Washington's rising sun chair, where he sat to oversee the Constitutional Convention

Washington and other **Patriot** leaders had high hopes for America, but there were many challenges to overcome. Division and lack of trust were problems throughout the young nation. Each state acted as if it were its own country.

If the states did not unite, the nation would fail. Washington saw the warning signs. Early in 1787, he and others traveled to Philadelphia to help write a new set of laws that would bind the country together.

As he had during the war, Washington continued to offer a steady hand. He directed events while sitting in a wooden chair carved with the face of a half-sun. When it was Washington's turn to sign the United States' new **constitution**, Benjamin Franklin looked at the carving and said, "I have the happiness to know that it is a rising and not a setting sun."

What happened in Philadelphia in 1787 was nothing short of a miracle. It gave hope to a growing nation and the world.

Delegates to the Constitutional Convention worked to create a document that would guide the young United States.

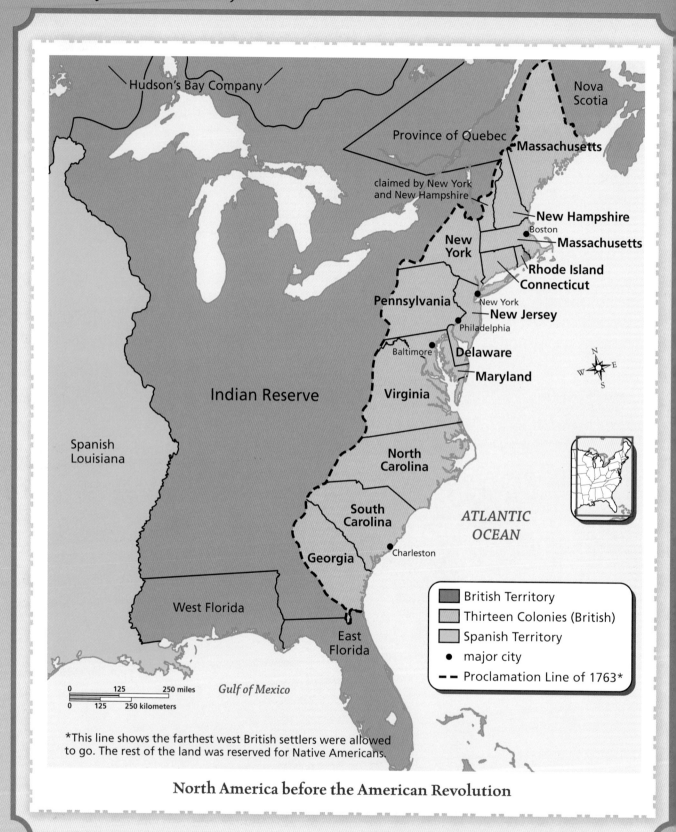

Hudson's Bay Company

Nova Scotia

Province of Quebec

Massachusetts

claimed by New York and New Hampshire

New Hampshire

Boston

New York

Massachusetts

Rhode Island

Connecticut

Pennsylvania

New York

New Jersey

Philadelphia

Baltimore

Delaware

Maryland

Indian Reserve

Virginia

Spanish Louisiana

North Carolina

South Carolina

ATLANTIC OCEAN

Georgia

Charleston

West Florida

East Florida

Gulf of Mexico

| 0 | 125 | 250 miles |
| 0 | 125 | 250 kilometers |

British Territory

Thirteen Colonies (British)

Spanish Territory

• major city

– – Proclamation Line of 1763*

*This line shows the farthest west British settlers were allowed to go. The rest of the land was reserved for Native Americans.

North America before the American Revolution

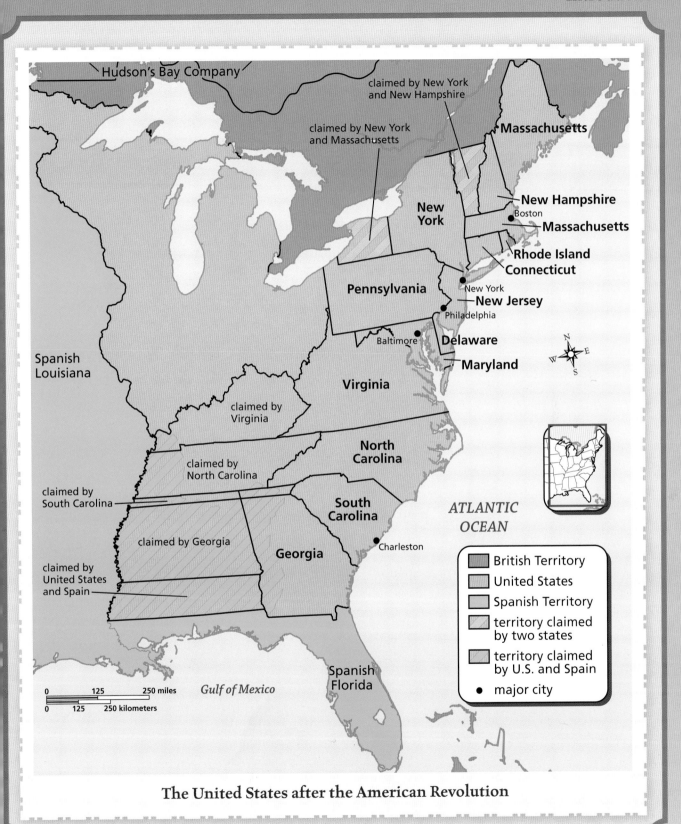

Hudson's Bay Company

claimed by New York
and New Hampshire

claimed by New York
and Massachusetts

Massachusetts

New York

New Hampshire

Boston

Massachusetts

Rhode Island
Connecticut

Pennsylvania

New York

New Jersey

Philadelphia

Spanish
Louisiana

Baltimore

Delaware

Maryland

Virginia

claimed by
Virginia

**North
Carolina**

claimed by
North Carolina

claimed by
South Carolina

**South
Carolina**

claimed by Georgia

Georgia

Charleston

**ATLANTIC
OCEAN**

claimed by
United States
and Spain

0   125   250 miles
0   125   250 kilometers

Gulf of Mexico

Spanish
Florida

	British Territory
	United States
	Spanish Territory
	territory claimed by two states
	territory claimed by U.S. and Spain
●	major city

The United States after the American Revolution

Freedom Around the Corner

Major Events

1777
Articles of Confederation written

1781
March 1
Articles of Confederation ratified

October 19
British surrender at Yorktown

1783
September 3
Treaty of Paris signed

October 17, 1781, was not a good day for British Lord Charles Cornwallis. Six years had passed since the first shots of the Revolutionary War were fired from Lexington and Concord. Now, the war was very close to its end.

Surrender at Yorktown

Cornwallis saw no escape as he looked out across Yorktown, a seaside village in Virginia. In front of him were the Continental Army and hundreds of French troops. Behind him sat the French navy. Cornwallis had hoped **reinforcements** would arrive to help him. They never did. Surrender was his only option.

Cornwallis reluctantly sent one of his officers across the battle lines to talk to Washington about the terms of surrender. Two days later, the British laid down their arms.

Cornwallis refused to attend the surrender ceremony. He did not want to hand over his sword to Washington, which was the custom for surrendering at that time. Instead, Cornwallis sent his next in command to turn over his sword. The British defeat at Yorktown effectively ended the war.

Surrender at Yorktown

Peace Talks

The Patriots had expected this day. They had already formed a peace **commission**. The American Congress had asked Benjamin Franklin, John Adams, Thomas Jefferson, John Jay, and several others to **negotiate** a formal peace **treaty**. Both sides began meeting in Paris in the fall of 1782.

On September 3, 1783, the United States and Great Britain signed the Treaty of Paris, officially ending the Revolutionary War. The agreement called for all British troops to leave the new United States. Britain also recognized American independence. As such, the United States officially owned the land from the Atlantic Ocean to the Mississippi River. The United States was also given permission to use the coast of Nova Scotia, Canada, for fishing. In return, the United States agreed to pay off all its colonial debts and protect the rights of American **Loyalists**.

As part of the Treaty of Paris, Britain made agreements with France and Spain, as well. Britain gave Florida to Spain but kept its Canadian territory. France was given British areas in the Caribbean and West Africa.

News of the treaty reached the United States with joyous celebration. Cannons boomed. Fireworks exploded. "To the United States!" Americans toasted, raising glasses of wine and beer. "To General Washington! To the American Army!"

No one in Britain believed the Americans could unite and create a government that worked, but the young nation of Patriots was up to the challenge.

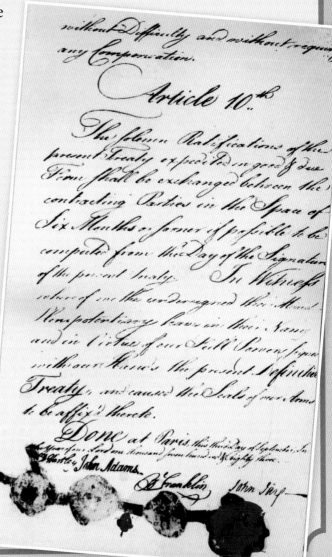

Treaty of Paris (1783)

What Do You Know!

The Continental Congress began working on a form of government for the independent colonies in June 1776. Each state also wrote its own governing document by 1780. Congress finished their Articles of Confederation on November 1, 1777, but it took three more years for all 13 states to ratify the Articles. The Articles went into effect on March 1, 1781.

A New Government

The American Revolution was unlike any conflict before it. The Americans had not only **overthrown** a **monarch**, but also formed a system of self-government. It was called **republicanism**. In a republic, people make their own decisions through **representatives** they have elected.

When the United States' founders signed the Declaration of Independence in 1776, each state thought of itself as a separate republic. They thought a strong **central government** would be too much like Britain's government.

Articles of Confederation

However, the states agreed to be bound together by the **Articles of Confederation**. This document was more like a treaty among states than a constitution. Each state kept "its **sovereignty**, freedom, and independence." The Articles were originally written in 1777, although the states did not formally **ratify** them until individual states' differences were resolved in 1781.

Smaller states did not like how the Articles handled **land claims** in the West. Some states were still competing with each other to extend their western borders. Smaller states, like Maryland and Delaware, wanted the larger states, like Georgia and New York, to give up their western land claims. However, the other states eventually convinced the smaller states that having some kind of compromise in place was better than having no national government at all. Finally, all the states agreed to ratify the Articles.

The states also delayed ratifying the Articles of Confederation because of their negative experience with the strong central government of Britain. Most Americans did not want to create another central government that had enough power to become a tyrant. Their experience with Britain's government had led to bloodshed. Americans believed the best way to protect individual liberty was to have a weak central government that would not interfere in the lives of citizens. That is exactly what the Articles did.

More Problems

The Articles created more problems than were solved. The Confederation Congress had little power. Its members rarely showed up for work. It could not raise taxes. It had no authority to set up a court system. It could not regulate trade or form an army. Laws had to be approved by at least nine of the 13 states. And **amendments** had to be approved **unanimously**. More importantly, Congress could not force the states to act for the common good.

No money, no troops, and not being able to make decisions for the good of the nation was a recipe for disaster. Farmers went broke. The nation's debt soared. The United States could not even protect itself.

Not Taken Seriously

To make matters worse, the monarchies of Europe had little respect for Americans and largely ignored The United States. Britain refused to send a government official to the United States. The British also failed to remove troops from the American northwest and along Lake Champlain in the northeast.

In the southwest, Spain declined to recognize American land claims. The Spanish closed parts of the Mississippi River to American **trade** and hoped to bring American settlers in Kentucky and Tennessee under their rule.

> **What Do You Think?**
> Why do you think Americans were nervous about having a strong central government?

Land Grab

As these and other problems mounted, American settlers pushed into the western frontier beyond the Appalachian Mountains. As the settlers **migrated**, land ownership disputes broke out between the states. Massachusetts and Virginia, for example, both claimed land west of the Ohio River. Massachusetts and New York claimed the same territory in western New York.

Something had to be done. Congress passed the Land Ordinance of 1785. The states ceded, or surrendered, the disputed territories to the federal government. Once the government took ownership, it put the land up for sale. Anyone could buy it. The ordinance cooled tensions between the bickering states.

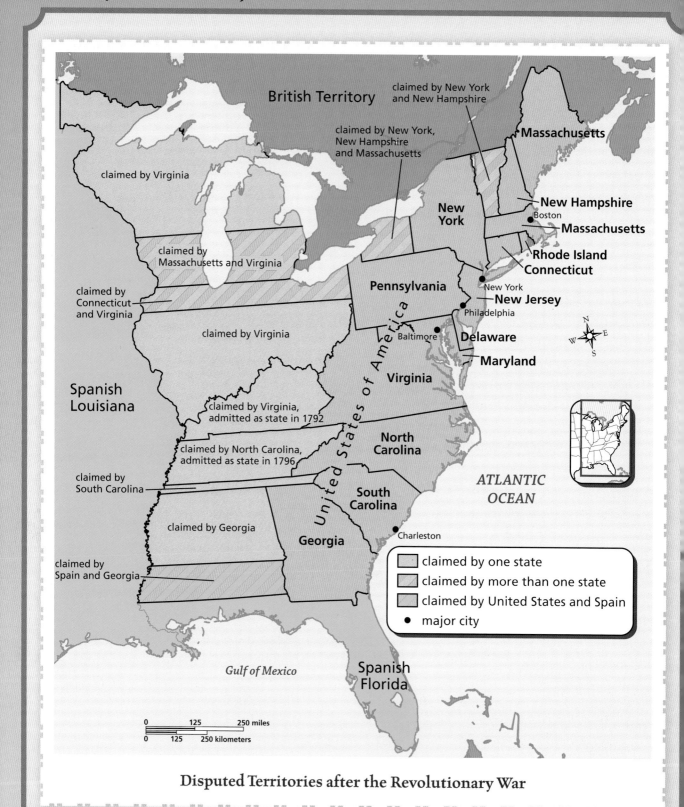

Disputed Territories after the Revolutionary War

Ohio Country

Two years later, the Northwest Ordinance of 1787 opened up land for development north of the Ohio River and east of the Mississippi River. The ordinance encouraged westward expansion. It also made slavery illegal in the Northwest. However, the ordinance allowed slavery to flourish in new territories and states south of the Ohio River.

Because the Confederation government was weak, the states mostly ignored these laws and other acts passed by Congress.

What Do You Know!

A central government is sometimes referred to as a national government or a federal government.

The Call Goes Out

The problems with the Articles of Confederation grew each day. The states imposed their own **duties** on goods **imported** from other states. New England's fishermen, whalers, and shipbuilders suffered because they could not find a **market** for their catch. Markets also dried up for Southern rice farmers and tobacco growers.

Some of the most successful men in the United States had lost faith with the Articles. George Washington said the Articles were "little more than the shadow without the substance." Charles Pinckney of South Carolina gave up on the Articles when Congress refused to act on a threat posed by the Spanish and Native Americans.

John Adams was another opponent of the Confederation Congress. He had been an active Patriot since the early days of the Revolution. Adams disliked that the Confederation Congress only had one assembly, or house of representatives. Most state legislatures had two assemblies of lawmakers, which Adams believed worked much better. Adams said if one assembly had all the power, "What was there to restrain [prevent] it from making tyrannical laws, in order to execute them in a tyrannical manner?"

> *[O]ur contest is not only whether we ourselves shall be free, but whether there shall be left to mankind an asylum on earth for civil and religious liberty.*
>
> —Samuel Adams

Mount Vernon, George Washington's home and meeting site for Virginia and Maryland representatives

What to Do?

No one argued that the Articles of Confederation limited growth, **commerce**, and **defense**. Still, changing the Articles would not be easy. James Madison had to try. He and several other Virginians, along with a group from Maryland, traveled to Washington's home in Mount Vernon. They wanted to discuss ways of improving **navigation** on the Potomac River.

The delegates looked out over the sprawling river and saw "a common High Way." They agreed on many issues. They settled fishing rights and how each state should enforce the law. They even agreed on where to build lighthouses. The Mount Vernon meeting went so well that the delegates decided to have a larger meeting in Annapolis, Maryland, in September 1786.

Annapolis Convention

Five states sent delegates, or representatives, to the Annapolis Convention. Once again, they all complained about the shortcomings of the Articles. They grumbled that the central government had no power to deal with national issues. Alexander Hamilton from New York, who had been a military aide to George Washington, used the meeting to call for a national convention in Philadelphia to "cement the union."

Congress had to agree before such an important meeting could take place. Getting Congress to go along would be difficult. But in the autumn of 1786, a former army captain named Daniel Shays gave Congress the reason it needed.

Shays's Rebellion

By the winter of 1786–1787, thousands of farmers in western Massachusetts were going broke. Unlike other states, Massachusetts did not forgive their debts. Instead, local sheriffs seized family farms and imprisoned those who could not pay their bills. The farmers were more than upset. Some staged an **uprising** in the fall of 1786 to show their anger. Their goal was to shut down the courts and prevent the trial and imprisonment of **debt-ridden** citizens.

Things snowballed quickly when a former army captain took charge of the rebellion. Daniel Shays fought during the American Revolution at the battles of Ticonderoga and Bunker Hill. On a freezing January day in 1787, nearly 2,000 New England farmers led by Shays tried to seize an **arsenal** at Springfield, Massachusetts.

The governor of Massachusetts, James Bowdoin, ordered the **militia** to put down the rebellion. The militia's cannons scattered the mob. Shays fled to Vermont. Still, the underlying causes of the revolt remained. Farmers and others staged similar rebellions in Connecticut, New York, Pennsylvania, and elsewhere.

This satirical drawing from 1787 shows anti-federalists leading Connecticut to a stormy land. One anti-federalist wishes, "Success to Shays!"

A New Constitution

Major Events

1787

May 25
Constitutional Convention begins

July 16
Great Compromise reached

September
Constitutional Convention ends

Independence Hall, Philadelphia

T he United States was being torn apart. Fears of lawlessness spread. On February 21, 1787, with Shays' Rebellion still fresh, Congress agreed to hold a convention "for the sole and express purpose of revising the Articles of Confederation."

On to Philadelphia

George Washington was the most respected man in the United States in 1787. He had suffered eight long years leading the Continental Army against the British. He spent his fortune and put his reputation on the line when it seemed the American cause would fail. Everyone in America knew what Washington had sacrificed. When he was invited to the Philadelphia convention, Washington did not want to go. He did not believe he had anything to contribute to the discussion. Yet, the former general reluctantly accepted the invitation. He knew his absence would harm the meeting.

Washington arrived in Philadelphia with Virginia's **delegation** on May 13, 1787. He wore the finest suit, and his wig was freshly powdered. Washington entered the city with church bells ringing and cannons booming.

Delegations from every state—with the exception of Rhode Island—soon arrived. The attendees included many prominent figures of the day including James Madison, Benjamin Franklin, Charles Pinckney, and John Rutledge.

Benjamin Franklin

Madison's Vision

Washington's presence gave the Philadelphia convention its authority. James Madison provided its soul. Madison was a 36-year-old representative from Virginia. He had helped write Virginia's Constitution and brought many ideas to the Constitutional Convention. Madison knew if the United States were to survive, it had to have a completely new set of laws. He also knew that most of the convention's delegates did not want to take such a step.

Growth to Ensure Prosperity

Madison came to Philadelphia armed with compelling arguments for a constitutional makeover. Madison believed a strong central government would create a larger union. He argued the larger the republic grew, the more it would prosper.

Madison also believed a strong central government could act as a referee between the states. A new constitution, he said, would create a "disinterested & dispassionate umpire in disputes between different passions & interests."

> A sincere and steadfast co-operation in promoting such a reconstruction of our political system as would provide for the permanent liberty and happiness of the United States.
>
> —James Madison

Debate Begins

What would be later known as the Constitutional Convention got underway on May 25, 1787. Its first order of business was to elect a chairman. The delegates unanimously picked Washington. The delegates also decided to hold hearings in secret. The delegates hoped the secrecy would allow honest discussions and arguments. It also protected the delegates from outside political pressures.

It quickly became clear the Articles of Confederation needed to be replaced. This went against Congress's original mandate. Still, most delegates believed a new constitution was the only thing that could save the union.

George Washington served as chairman of the Constitutional Convention. His presence and leadership helped unite the various factions of the convention.

Three Branches of Government

The Convention soon decided to create a republican government, meaning that people would elect representatives to govern for them. For the American Republic, the Convention designed three branches—the **legislative branch**, or Congress; the **executive branch**, or the Presidency; and the **judicial branch**, or the courts. The delegates thought having three branches of government would prevent anyone from becoming too powerful. They wanted to avoid a government that seemed like a monarchy.

> *If men were angels, no government would be necessary.*
>
> —James Madison

The delegates began the legislative branch, or Congress. Edmund Randolph of Virginia stood before the convention on May 29 and proposed the Virginia Plan. The plan's 15 resolutions created a **bicameral** legislature. Lawmakers in the lower house of Congress would elect the upper house in order to make sure the best people were in charge. The lower house would pick the country's president and judges. The lower house could nullify, or do away with, state laws. It could also admit new states into the union.

 What Do You Know!

The Constitutional Convention met from May 25 to September 17, 1787 at Independence Hall in Philadelphia. There were 55 delegates from every state except Rhode Island. The convention wrote the seven articles that make up the current U.S. Constitution. In the end, only 39 delegates ended up signing the finished Constitution. The rest decided to abstain because they were not sure about the document. The convention was contentious, or highly debated, but successful.

Concerns about the Virginia Plan

The Virginia Plan was controversial. It gave a lot of power to one group of legislators. It also gave the more **populous** states, such as Virginia, more representatives in Congress than the smaller states. The Virginia Plan became known as the "large state plan."

Fighting Factions

Randolph's proposal split the convention. Each **faction** protected its own interest. The smaller states wanted a strong central government. They feared the larger states would bully and dominate them. Slave states battled with those states that opposed slavery. Some states did not want to a give a new Congress control over commerce. For example, New York filled its treasury by collecting custom duties at its ports. New York feared a stronger government would end this.

The delegates battled for two weeks. To break the political deadlock, William Patterson of New Jersey offered a plan written by the New Jersey delegation. Like the Virginia Plan, the so-called New Jersey Plan gave Congress sweeping powers. It also created a **unicameral** legislature, in which each "sovereign" state had one vote.

The Great Compromise

Madison and others blasted the New Jersey Plan. They said the states were not sovereign units. Washington was tired of hearing the word "sovereign." He called it a "monster." Alexander Hamilton offered a proposal of his own—a bicameral legislature with an elected lower house of representatives. Those in the upper house, or Senate, would serve for life.

The convention had become hopelessly deadlocked as Philadelphia baked under a hot summer sun. Arguments broke out. Crowds waited outside for news. The windows to the convention hall were shut tight so word of what was happening did not spill out. The convention was crumbling.

Ingenious Solution

Finally, Roger Sherman and the rest of the Connecticut delegation offered an **ingenious**, solution. Their "Connecticut Plan," or "Connecticut Compromise," divided Congress into two houses. Each state, no matter its size, would have an equal number of representatives in the Senate. Membership in a House of Representatives would be based on the population of each state. To gather Southern support, slaves counted as three-fifths of a person.

Roger Sherman

People at the Time

Roger Sherman

Roger Sherman was born on April 19, 1721, in Newton, Massachusetts. He was admitted to the bar, meaning he became a lawyer, in 1754 in Connecticut. He was an elected representative to the Connecticut House in the 1760s and 1770s. He helped craft the Constitution. He served as senator for Connecticut from 1791 until his death in 1793.

The Divided Convention

Debating

The delegates had to decide what to do. The smaller states did not like the idea of counting slaves. That would give the Southern states more power in the House.

Washington, sitting in the chair carved with the face of the half-sun, kept the debate from getting out of control. He scheduled a vote on the Connecticut Plan for July 16. He called the roll of states. New Hampshire and Rhode Island were absent. New York lacked a **quorum** and could not vote yes or no. The Massachusetts's delegation split over what to do. Connecticut and New Jersey voted for the compromise. Delaware and Maryland also voted yes. Pennsylvania voted no.

Finally a Decision

The balance hung with the Southern states. All were expected to reject the plan. They feared it created a central government that was too strong. The delegation from North Carolina had a different opinion. Its delegates voted with the smaller states. The measure passed. The convention had reached what was later called the "Great Compromise." The makeup of Congress was finally settled. Delegates began to agree on the remaining issues.

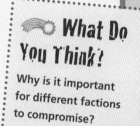

What Do You Think?

Why is it important for different factions to compromise?

Legislative Branch

As the summer days wore on, the delegates decided which specific powers Congress, or the legislative branch, should have. They wrote those powers down in Article I of the Constitution. Article I gave Congress the power to make laws. Congress could tax and declare war and they could settle disputes between the states. They could also regulate commerce and borrow money. Congress was designed with two houses, the House of Representatives and the Senate. Representatives were elected by the people every two years. Senators would be chosen by the state government every six years. The House of Representatives introduced laws, but the laws had to be approved by the Senate.

Executive Branch

The government needed someone to head the executive branch and enforce the laws Congress made. Edmund Randolph wanted Congress to pick the president because Congress represented the will of the people. Many opposed Randolph's proposal, fearing it would give Congress too much power. Alexander Hamilton raised more than a few eyebrows when he proposed giving the president the powers of a king. Still, others wanted the state legislatures to choose the nation's president.

After some debate, the delegates drafted Article II, which created the office of president and vice president. The Constitutional Convention did not want the chief executive, or president, to be directly elected. Instead, the states would vote for **electors**. These electors formed an Electoral College. The number of electors depended upon the total number of senators and representatives each state had. Article II also made the president the commander in chief of the military. Finally, the delegates drafted Article III. That Article set up the court system, or judicial branch, of government. This branch was led by the Supreme Court.

Checks and Balances

The delegates did not want one branch of government to dominate the others. Their solution was to create a system of **checks and balances**, in which the powers of the three branches of government overlapped. For example, Congress made the laws, but the president, head of the executive branch, had the power to **veto** them. However, Congress could override the president's veto with a two-thirds majority vote. Congress could also **impeach** and remove judges, or even the president, if they did not perform their duties.

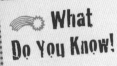

What Do You Know!

SEPARATION OF POWERS

The principle of separation of powers comes from the Roman era. The Roman Republic had an assembly, a Senate, and an executive consul. French philosopher Charles de Montesquieu developed the idea further during the Enlightenment in the 1700s. The framers of the U.S. Constitution thought separation of powers was the best way to prevent tyranny, or one person or branch becoming too powerful.

The president had the power to appoint judges and other government officials. However, the Senate had to approve those appointments. The Constitution also gave the president power to negotiate treaties with other nations. It was the Senate's job to approve those treaties.

The Constitution made the president the overall commander of the military. Only Congress could declare war. As for the Supreme Court, it could strike down any law passed by Congress if it determined the law **unconstitutional**. This is called judicial review.

> "
>
> *We the People of the United States, in Order to form a more perfect Union, establish Justice, insure domestic Tranquility, provide for the common defence, promote the general Welfare, and secure the Blessings of Liberty to ourselves and our Posterity, do ordain and establish this Constitution for the United States of America. . . .*
>
> —Preamble to the U.S. Constitution
>
> "

The Constitution

What Do You Know!

Why do you think the first three words of the Constitution are "We the People"?

The Constitution's Legacy

The delegates to the Constitutional Convention wrapped up their work in September 1787. The document was signed by 39 of the original 55 delegates. As the delegates stepped outside, a woman asked Benjamin Franklin, "What have you given us?" Franklin responded, "A Republic, madam, if you can keep it."

Despite its many shortcomings, the U.S. Constitution was an incredibly important document. It established for the first time a stable democratic government. Although originally written for a rural, farming society, the framers made sure the document could change with the times. Today it guides a population of more than 300 million people. The unique aspect of the Constitution is its system of checks and balances. As a result, when one branch of government falters, the other branches can pick up the slack.

The Issue of Slavery

The Constitution solved many problems, but was silent on one major issue—slavery. By the end of the Revolutionary War, many Northern states had begun the gradual **abolition** of slavery. Slavery in the South continued. Slaves were vital to the South's farming **economy**. If slave owners gave up their slaves, they would be giving up a lot of their wealth.

"Other Persons"

The issue of slavery hung over the Constitutional Convention like a summer thunderstorm. It had the ability to destroy all the delegates had accomplished. Not once was the word "slavery" mentioned in the new Constitution. The delegates used vague terms such as "other persons." Moreover, treating slaves as three-fifths of a person gave the slaveholding states extra representation in Congress and the Electoral College. The delegates agreed to allow the slave trade to continue until at least 1808. The issue of slavery in the United States was not settled until the Civil War. The Thirteenth Amendment outlawed slavery in 1865.

> " . . . [M]any important . . . Powers are vested in you [Congress] for 'promoting the Welfare & Securing the blessings of liberty to the People of the United States.' And . . . these blessings ought rightfully to be administered, without distinction of Colour, to all descriptions of People . . . . "
> —Benjamin Franklin in a letter to Congress, 1790

Why Allow Slavery?

Why did the framers of the Constitution ignore the issue of slavery? They did so because national unity was at stake. The framers thought states needed to forge a stronger bond and create a more powerful government. The writers of the Constitution did not want the issue of slavery to derail those plans. The issue also went to the heart of private property, which most Americans considered the cornerstone of liberty. Slaves were considered property at the time. In the minds of Americans in the 1700s, tampering with slavery was tampering with American rights to their property.

> "
> *The people made the Constitution, and the people can unmake it. It is the creature of their will, and lives only by their will.*
> —John Marshall, Chief Justice of the Supreme Court, 1821
> "

Enslaved people often picked cotton on plantations in the South.

The Great Debate

Major Events

1788

February 6
Massachusetts
ratifies Constitution

June 22
Virginia ratifies
Constitution

The Constitutional Convention was over. The delegates had reorganized America's government. But while the Constitution had been approved, only some delegates really supported it. The debate did not end when the delegates went home. It had only begun. The future of the Constitution was in the states' hands.

To the States

The Constitution could not become law unless the states approved. All 13 states had to ratify, or officially approve, the Constitution. However, the Constitution could go into effect with only nine states approval. Either way, it would not be easy. Most Americans were still unwilling to give more power to a central government. Each state was to hold a special convention with elected representatives. The delegates would then vote to approve the document. Delaware was the first to give its approval on December 7, 1787. Several smaller states followed because they felt the new Constitution gave them more power than the Articles of Confederation.

Across the country, people gathered in taverns and on street corners to voice their opinions. Support for the Constitution was low. Someone needed to sell it to the farmers, shopkeepers, **artisans**, lumberjacks, and fishermen across America. That job fell to Alexander Hamilton, James Madison, and John Jay.

Selling the Constitution

Alexander Hamilton was an American **icon**. He was from the West Indies. He came to America as the first whiffs of revolution filled the air and he caught the attention of George Washington. The general invited Hamilton to join his inner circle as an **aide-de-camp**, an honored position. Hamilton became a rich and popular attorney after the American Revolution ended. Most thought he was a legal genius. Although he took the lead in organizing the Constitutional Convention, Hamilton took a backseat in Philadelphia to James Madison and others. Now the time had come for Hamilton to take center stage once again.

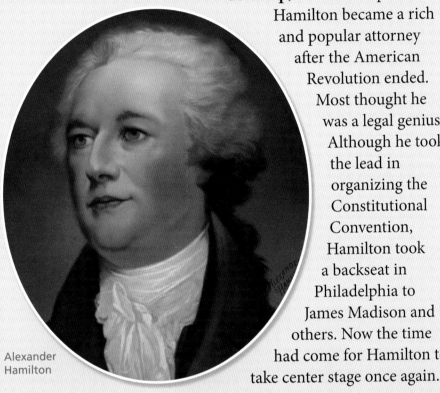

Alexander Hamilton

The Federalists

The Constitution was doomed without the support of the large states including Massachusetts, New York, and Virginia. So Hamilton, Jay, and Madison went on an advertising campaign of sorts. They wrote a series of 85 essays known as the *Federalist Papers*. Local newspapers printed the essays under the pen name "Publius." In the letters, Publius discussed why the Constitution was important. No one knew the identity of the writers.

> " *You must first enable the government to control the governed; and in the next place, oblige it to control itself.*
>
> —James Madison, the *Federalist Papers* "

Persuasive Writing

It was Hamilton's idea to write the essays. He hoped his arguments would win over his home state of New York. Hamilton feared the Constitution would die if his fellow New Yorkers did not approve the proposal.

Hamilton began the first essay by laying out the responsibility of each citizen. ". . . you are called upon to deliberate [seriously give thought to] on a new Constitution for the United States of America," Hamilton wrote. "The subject speaks its own importance; comprehending in its consequences nothing less than the existence of the UNION . . ."

He then laid out his arguments in a logical and practical way. The essays proved "a masterful piece of political spin," according to one historian. They persuaded the doubtful to ratify the Constitution. Today, people read the *Federalist Papers* when they want to understand the intention of the Constitution's framers.

> " *It has been frequently remarked . . . whether societies of men are really capable or not, of establishing good government from reflection and choice, or whether they are forever destined to depend, for their political constitutions, on accident and force.*
>
> —Alexander Hamilton, the *Federalist Papers* "

James Madison

Opposition

As people read the *Federalist* essays, a group opposing the Constitution took shape. Members of that group called themselves the **anti-federalists**. They favored a weak central government. Individual liberty was at the center of their argument. The anti-federalists said the Constitution did not guarantee individual freedoms, such as speech, assembly, and religion. They argued that these rights had to be spelled out so the government could not take them away.

The anti-federalists penned their own essays under the name "Brutus" and other **pseudonyms**. In those articles, known as the *Anti-Federalist Papers*, the authors urged the states to reject the Constitution.

Anti-Federalist Fears

The debate grew heated. Patrick Henry had previously pleaded with Americans to embrace independence in 1776. He now warned of the dangers of **tyranny**. "If a wrong step be now made, the republic may be lost forever." In Albany, New York, angry mobs burned copies of the Constitution.

Some anti-federalists complained that the document did not abolish the slave trade. Others believed the Constitution was a plot to make the rich wealthier. "These lawyers, and men of learning and moneyed men, that . . . make us poor illiterate people swallow down the pill . . . they will swallow up all us little folks like the great Leviathan [sea monster]," cried one anti-federalist.

Patrick Henry

People at the Time

John Hancock

John Hancock, who is mostly known for his large signature on the Declaration of Independence, was born in 1737 in Massachusetts. He was an important supporter of the Patriot cause and served as president of the Second Continental Congress during the Revolutionary War. He was then governor of Massachusetts. His vote was important in Massachusetts ratifying the Constitution. He died in 1793, four years after the Constitution was adopted.

Hancock, Once Again

John Hancock was a rich Boston merchant, a one-time smuggler, and beloved Patriot. He had been an important figure during the American Revolution. He was the first to sign the Declaration of Independence. Now Hancock had a more pressing issue. He tried to get his home state of Massachusetts to sign off on the Constitution.

Massachusetts and Virginia were two of the most influential states in the Union because of their population and size. The Massachusetts Ratification Convention began debating the issue on January 9, 1788. As the days passed, the convention remained at a standstill.

Finally, Hancock—the convention's president—made a promise. If the delegates voted for the Constitution, he would make sure it contained a bill of rights guaranteeing such privileges as freedom of speech and assembly. His announcement ended the stalemate. On February 6, Massachusetts voted in favor of the Constitution.

Hancock's call for a bill of rights pushed other states, including Virginia, to approve the Constitution. By mid-1788, nine states had voted for ratification. It was now the law of the land. Still, the document would not amount to much unless the remaining states came on board. By the spring of 1790, all 13 states approved the document.

> "
> *I congratulate you and my country on the singular favor of heaven in the peaceable and auspicious [lucky] settlement of our government upon a Constitution formed by wisdom, and sanctified by the solemn choice of the people who are to live under it.*
>
> —John Hancock, in a speech to the Massachusetts legislature
> "

America's Bill of Rights

In 1791, the new Congress formed a committee to draft a bill of rights. Heading that committee was James Madison. "A bill of rights is what the people are entitled to against every government on earth," Thomas Jefferson wrote Madison.

Madison was skeptical that such a declaration was necessary. Eventually he came around to the idea. Still, he called the task of drafting the bill a "nauseous project."

Such a declaration was not only a distinctive American idea. Other countries had similar documents. The British had the Magna Carta and the English Bill of Rights, which, among other things, guaranteed freedom of speech. Virginia's Declaration of Rights declared in 1776, that "all men by nature are equally free and independent and have certain inherent rights."

Amendments to the Constitution

Madison's committee finished its work. Congress agreed to add ten amendments to the Constitution—the Bill of Rights. Those amendments guaranteed Americans many freedoms, including religion, speech, press, assembly, and petition in the First Amendment. Americans also had the right to own weapons and a trial by jury according to the Second Amendment.

The Ninth Amendment let everyone know the Bill of Rights was not a complete list. It said Americans had rights beyond those stated in the Constitution. Once again, the states had to approve the changes. By December 15, 1791, three-fourths of the states had ratified the Bill of Rights. Over the years, Americans would add more than a dozen amendments to the Constitution.

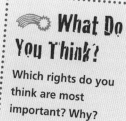

What Do You Think?

Which rights do you think are most important? Why?

> **[T]he freedom of Speech may be taken away, and dumb and silent we may be led, like sheep, to the Slaughter.**
>
> —George Washington

The right to protest today is protected under the first amendment.

THE BILL OF RIGHTS

Amendment I
Congress shall make no law respecting an establishment of religion, or prohibiting the free exercise thereof; or abridging the freedom of speech, or of the press; or the right of the people peaceably to assemble, and to petition the Government for a redress of grievances.

Amendment II
A well regulated Militia, being necessary to the security of a free State, the right of the people to keep and bear Arms, shall not be infringed.

Amendment III
No Soldier shall, in time of peace be quartered in any house, without the consent of the Owner, nor in time of war, but in a manner to be prescribed by law.

Amendment IV
The right of the people to be secure in their persons, houses, papers, and effects, against unreasonable searches and seizures, shall not be violated, and no Warrants shall issue, but upon probable cause, supported by Oath or affirmation, and particularly describing the place to be searched, and the persons or things to be seized.

Amendment V
No person shall be held to answer for a capital, or otherwise infamous crime, unless on a presentment or indictment of a Grand Jury, except in cases arising in the land or naval forces, or in the Militia, when in actual service in time of War or public danger; nor shall any person be subject for the same offence to be twice put in jeopardy of life or limb; nor shall be compelled in any criminal case to be a witness against himself, nor be deprived of life, liberty, or property, without due process of law; nor shall private property be taken for public use, without just compensation.

Amendment VI

In all criminal prosecutions, the accused shall enjoy the right to a speedy and public trial, by an impartial jury of the State and district wherein the crime shall have been committed, which district shall have been previously ascertained by law, and to be informed of the nature and cause of the accusation; to be confronted with the witnesses against him; to have compulsory process for obtaining witnesses in his favor, and to have the Assistance of Counsel for his defence.

Amendment VII

In Suits at common law, where the value in controversy shall exceed twenty dollars, the right of trial by jury shall be preserved, and no fact tried by a jury, shall be otherwise re-examined in any Court of the United States, than according to the rules of the common law.

Amendment VIII

Excessive bail shall not be required, nor excessive fines imposed, nor cruel and unusual punishments inflicted.

Amendment IX

The enumeration in the Constitution, of certain rights, shall not be construed to deny or disparage others retained by the people.

Amendment X

The powers not delegated to the United States by the Constitution, nor prohibited by it to the States, are reserved to the States respectively, or to the people.

Changes or challenges to an amendment are made in a court of law.

"

In Europe, charters of liberty have been granted by power. America has set the example . . . of charters of power granted by liberty. This revolution in the practice of the world, may, with an honest praise, be pronounced the most triumphant epoch of its history, and the most consoling presage of its happiness.

—James Madison, 1792

"

Governing in a Free Land

Major Events

1789

April 30
Washington inaugurated as president

September 24
Congress passes Judiciary Act

The Constitutional Convention was over. George Washington was finally home. He had first left his beloved Mount Vernon estate to help win a war. He left again to build a nation. Now it was time to lead the country.

The Nation's Father

Charles Thomson knocked on Washington's door with a letter in his hand. The note invited Washington to New York City, the new capital of the United States. The letter said that the Electoral College had unanimously elected Washington as the nation's first president. John Adams was elected as his vice president.

Washington's inauguration

Washington read the letter with excitement and despair. He did not want to leave Mount Vernon. As other times in his life, duty called. He prepared for his trip with a heavy, but grateful heart. He made sure the estate was in order for his wife Martha. He rode off for New York to attend his **inauguration** with mixed emotions. "About ten o'clock I bade farewell to Mount Vernon, to private life, and to domestic felicity [happiness]," he wrote.

Washington Steps Up

Washington arrived in New York eight days later. It would have been much sooner. Celebrations slowed his journey. Huge crowds greeted Washington along the way with bonfires, fireworks, and speeches.

On April 30, 1789, Washington stood on the balcony of Federal Hall on Wall Street and took the **oath of office**. Washington was now at the center of the world's greatest experiment in democracy.

What to Do?

No one had ever held the job of president of the United States before. There was no roadmap for Washington to follow, no person to guide him. Washington knew his actions would set a **precedent**. He would be an example that future presidents would follow. Washington believed it was important that everyone respect the office of president. He dressed in fine clothes. He rode in a yellow carriage pulled by six well-groomed white horses.

The Constitution gave Washington the power to appoint advisers. He called these helpers "secretaries." They became part of Washington's **cabinet**. The president asked Thomas Jefferson to be secretary of state. Jefferson was to help Washington deal with other nations. Washington picked Alexander Hamilton as secretary of the treasury. Hamilton was to organize the nation's **monetary** system. Henry Knox was Washington's secretary of war. Knox was an old friend who served as Washington's chief of **artillery** during the Revolutionary War. Washington picked about 350 people to help him run the executive branch.

George Washington and his Cabinet

Virginia Dynasty

Virginia is the land of presidents. In fact, four of the first five presidents of the United States came from Virginia. They were Washington, Jefferson, Madison, and James Monroe.

The Virginia Dynasty, as it was called, showed the world that although the Southern states and Northern states had major differences, each was committed to a democratic union. The point was emphasized when leaders decided in 1790 to relocate the capital to a spot on the Potomac River across from Virginia. The city was later named Washington.

Establishing a Court System

As Washington got to work, so did the new Congress. One of its first actions was to create a federal court system. Congress passed the Judiciary Act of 1789. The law created 13 district courts and three circuit courts. In a circuit court, judges hold session in different locations.

Congress decided the federal courts would serve mainly as courts of **appeal** for cases already tried in local courts. Lawmakers feared federal courts would have too much power over local courts. Under this new system, however, a local judge was the first to hear a case. The case could then be appealed to a state court, or if necessary, a federal court.

The Judiciary Act also allowed Congress to determine the makeup of the Supreme Court, the highest court in the land. Lawmakers decided the Supreme Court would have six justices, or judges.

> *But our society—unlike most in the world—presupposes that freedom and liberty are in a frame of reference that makes the individual, not government, the keeper of his tastes, beliefs, and ideas; that is the philosophy of the First Amendment; and it is this article of faith that sets us apart from most nations in the world.*
>
> —Supreme Court Justice William O. Douglas

What Do You Know!

The Judicial Act of 1789 created a Supreme Court of six justices. After that, the number of justices went up and down between five and ten justices. In 1869 the number of justices was fixed at nine, the same number we have today. Currently, there are three women and six men on the Supreme Court. Sandra Day O'Connor became the first female justice in 1981.

Party Time

It didn't take long for problems to surface in the new government. Jefferson and Hamilton clashed with one another over various policies. Both men were smart. Each had the nation's best interests in mind. The fighting created stress for Washington and his cabinet.

"Mr. Jefferson," Hamilton wrote, "is the head of a faction decidedly hostile to me [a group that thinks he's an enemy] and dangerous to the union, peace, and the happiness of the country."

Jefferson said Hamilton's plans were "calculated [designed] to undermine and demolish the Republic."

The First Political Parties

Jefferson and Hamilton each led a faction of followers. Those factions became the country's first political parties. Those who followed Jefferson called themselves the "Democratic-Republicans," or Republicans. Hamilton's followers formed the "Federalist Party."

Washington did not like the idea of political parties. He said they stirred up "the community with ill-founded jealousies and false alarms." Madison, however, said political parties were good for the country. Competing parties stopped each other from having too much power.

Why did Hamilton and Jefferson disagree? Hamilton believed the government should be strong. He said only the rich and well-educated should hold power. Jefferson feared a powerful government would harm individual freedoms. He believed ordinary people could govern themselves.

Thomas Jefferson

The Nation's Money

The two mainly argued about money—the nation's money. Hamilton wanted the United States to be strong. He said people at home and in other countries had to have confidence in the new nation's economic system. He proposed the United States pay back all the money—$67 million—that it borrowed during the Revolution, with **interest**. It was known as "debt at par." Hamilton said such a move would signal that the United States could be trusted to meet its financial **obligations**. Hamilton said his proposals would unite the states.

Hamilton also proposed that Congress set taxes on **liquor** to pay its debts. Opponents argued the taxes would harm farmers who used their grain to make liquor. Congressmen from farming states in the South believed Hamilton's scheme would make businessmen in the North rich. In 1790, lawmakers reached a compromise. Congress agreed to pay off the debt and collect an **excise tax** as long as the nation's capital moved south to the District of Columbia.

Federalists and Republicans **quarrel**

Alexander Hamilton got his national bank in 1791 when Congress chartered the Bank of the United States. Today it is known as the Federal Reserve.

Bank on It

Jefferson did not like Hamilton's policies. Jefferson and others believed the new government should ignore the debts of the old government. Jefferson also disagreed with Hamilton over the creation of a national bank. Jefferson thought states should charter banks that could issue money. Hamilton wanted the bank to store the government's money and direct its finances.

Strict versus Loose Constructionists

The national bank debate highlighted the differing views over how people should interpret the Constitution. Jefferson was a "strict **constructionist**." He believed the government held only those powers that were specifically written in the Constitution. Hamilton was a "loose constructionist." He believed the Constitution could be interpreted as allowing anything that was not mentioned as forbidden. Ultimately, George Washington sided with Hamilton. Congress created the national bank.

Industrial Might

The two men were also at odds over the role **manufacturing** should play in the United States. By expanding America's industrial base, Hamilton believed the nation would become more financially stable. Again, Jefferson disagreed. He believed that farming was the key to American success.

The American Legacy

The American Revolution changed the course of history. The Declaration of Independence and the Constitution were examples of a change in world thinking.

Major Events

1775–1783

American Revolution against Great Britain

1789

French Revolution against monarch and nobles

1798

Irish Rebellion for self-rule against Great Britain unsuccessful

1810–1821

Mexican War of Independence against Spain

A Worldwide Impact

Many famous **philosophers**, like John Locke and Jean-Jacques Rousseau, wrote about people in a new way during the Enlightenment of the 1700s. They wrote about freedom and individual rights. These philosophers' ideas can be clearly seen in the United States' founding documents.

Government of the People and for the People

The Constitution was unique. Never before had a country been founded with specific rights and powers written down. Other countries had developed their laws as they went along. Since the writing of the U.S. Constitution, many other nations have written their constitutions so that governments cannot take advantage of the people. The world of all-powerful rulers shifted with the American Revolution. In the United States, the power now rested with the people.

Americans were not the only ones to embrace this new thinking. Around the world, people were beginning to think that monarchs and **absolute rule** was wrong. Just a few short years after the colonies united to overthrow a powerful government, the French people rose up against their oppressive leaders.

Another Revolution

Marie Antoinette awoke on the morning of October 16, 1793, and rubbed the sleep from her eyes. Nine months had passed since the revolutionaries of France sent her husband, King Louis XVI, to the **guillotine**. This would be the day of her **execution**.

King Louis XVI had **inherited** a country deep in debt when he took the throne in 1774. The problems only got worse during his **reign**. Encouraged by the success of the American Revolution, the French took to the streets and demanded change. The crowd shouted "Vive la Republique!"—French for Long Live the Republic!—as the blade came down on the queen.

The fight for American independence would also spur similar revolts in later years in Asia, Latin America, and other countries. Many have said America is not just a place, but an idea.

The **ideals** of the American Revolution and the U.S. Constitution still speak to a great many people today. Its principles are at the forefront of many movements across the globe where people yearn to be free.

French Revolution

GLOSSARY

abolition ending or making illegal; especially a negative practice

absolute rule the complete and unlimited political power of a ruler over his or her people

aide-de-camp a military officer acting as a confidential assistant to a general or senior officer

amendments changes to an existing document in order to improve that document

anti-federalists those who opposed ratification of the U.S. Constitution or a strong central government

appeal to ask a judge in a higher court to take a second look at a legal decision

arsenal a place, generally a building, where weapons and military equipment are stored

Articles of Confederation a set of laws that governed the United States before the Constitution was created; emphasized state power and limited central authority

artillery large guns, such as cannons

artisans skilled craftspeople

bicameral law-making body consisting of two parts or houses

cabinet a group of people who act as advisers to important government officials

cement to make stronger bonds between people

central government the government of the whole country or nation

checks and balances a system built into the U.S. Constitution in which the power of one branch of government is restrained by the other two branches

commerce the large-scale buying and selling of goods and services

commission directed to perform a duty; a group of people who have been given the authority to perform special duties

constitution a written set of basic laws or principles by which a country is governed

constructionist a person who analyzes and interprets laws in a specific way

debt-ridden owing a large amount of money, services, or goods

defense protection against attack; [in court] the person accused of doing something wrong, and his or her lawyer

delegation a group of people chosen to represent or act on behalf of somebody else

duties a tax on imported or exported goods

economy a country's financial system

electors people who vote to choose a candidate for a government office

excise tax a domestic tax on goods

execution killing someone as a legal punishment for a crime

executive branch the branch of government that carries out laws; the U.S. president, cabinet, and departments that carry out the law

faction a group of individuals within a larger group

guillotine a machine for executing people by beheading

icon a famous person or object that represents something of importance; an image that is godly or sacred

ideals the values or beliefs that a person thinks are most important

impeach to formally accuse a public official of a crime in connection with their job; to remove a person from political office because of misconduct

imported brought in from another country

inauguration the formal act of placing somebody in an official position, such as the president of the United States

ingenious a skilled or inventive way to do something or to solve a problem

inherited to have received something after the former owner leaves or dies

interest an extra cost that someone pays in order to borrow money

investors a person or company that has placed money in something

judicial branch the branch of government that is responsible for the country's legal system; all the judges in the country's courts of law

land claims the demand or request to legally control areas of property

legislative branch the branch of government that makes laws and collects taxes; the U.S. Congress

liquor a beverage that is made of alcohol

Loyalists Americans who supported the British during the Revolutionary War

manufacturing the producing of goods in factories

market the demand for products or services; an area or group that goods can be sold to

migrated having moved to a different area

militia a small military unit made up of citizens; usually used only in emergency

monarch the hereditary, or family-inherited, ruler of a nation or people

monetary having to do with money

navigation directing the course of a ship, or other vehicle

negotiate to talk over and arrange terms for an agreement

oath of office the ceremony to accept a job in government with an official promise to serve the country

obligations things one has to do

overthrow to remove from power by force

Patriot one who desired independence for the American colonies from Great Britain

philosophers thinkers who seek wisdom and knowledge

populous having a lot of people living in an area or place

precedent a standard that has been set before

pseudonym a fake name, generally used by writers

quarrel to argue about something; an angry disagreement

quorum a fixed minimum or number of members of a legislative assembly, committee, or other organization that must be present before the members can conduct valid business

ratify to give formal approval to something

reign to rule a country; to have power or control

reinforcements the addition of troops during a battle or conflict

representatives the people chosen to speak for others

republicanism the belief that the supreme power of a nation should be vested in its electorate

sovereignty a politically independent state

surrender to give up or lay down arms

trade to buy or sell goods; the business of buying and selling

treaty an official agreement between two or more countries that is formally approved and signed by their leaders

tyranny a government in which a ruler has all the power; cruel use of power over others

unanimously having the agreement of all

unconstitutional not allowed by or against the principles set down in the constitution

unicameral law-making body made up of one group of elected officials

uprising a sometimes violent act of opposition by a group of people against those in power

veto to not allow laws proposed by another branch of government to pass

TIMELINE

1775	April	Revolutionary War begins
1777		Articles of Confederation written
1781	March 1	Articles of Confederation ratified
	October 19	British surrender at Yorktown
1783	September 3	Treaty of Paris signed
1787	May 25	Constitutional Convention begins
	July 16	Great Compromise reached
	September	Constitutional Convention ends
1788	February 6	Massachusetts ratifies Constitution
	June 22	Virginia ratifies Constitution
1789	April 30	Washington inaugurated as President
	September 24	Congress passes the Judiciary Act
	July 14	French Revolution against monarch and nobles begins
1798		Irish rebellion for self-rule against Great Britain unsuccessful
1810–1821		Mexican War of Independence from Spain

FURTHER READING AND WEBSITES

Books

Aloian, Molly. *George Washington: Hero of the American Revolution*. Crabtree Publishing Company, 2013.

Aloian, Molly. *Phillis Wheatley: Poet of the Revolutionary Era*. Crabtree Publishing Company, 2013.

Bowman, David. *What Would the Founding Fathers Think?* Cedar Fort, Inc., 2012.

Clarke, Gordon. *Significant Battles of the American Revolution*. Crabtree Publishing Company, 2013.

Cocca, Lisa Colozza. *Marquis de Lafayette: Fighting for America's Freedom*. Crabtree Publishing Company, 2013.

Jordan, Terry L. *The U.S. Constitution And Fascinating Facts About It*. Oak Hill Publishing, 1999.

Kozak, Ellen M. *The Everything U.S. Constitution Book: An easy-to-understand explanation of the foundation of American government (Everything Series)*. Adams Media, 2011.

Mason, Helen. *Life on the Homefront during the American Revolution*. Crabtree Publishing Company, 2013.

Perritano, John. *The Causes of the American Revolution*. Crabtree Publishing Company, 2013.

Roberts, Steve. *King George III: England's Struggle to Keep America*. Crabtree Publishing Company, 2013.

Turner, Juliette. *Our Constitution Rocks*. Zondervan, 2012.

Websites

"Constitution of the United States." *Charters of Freedom*.
http://www.archives.gov/exhibits/charters/constitution.html

"Meet George Washington." *Mount Vernon*.
http://www.mountvernon.org/meetgeorge-washington

"James Madison."
http://www.history.com/topics/james-madison

BIBLIOGRAPHY

Davenport, John. *The American Revolution.* Lucent Books, 2007.

Langguth, A.J. *The Men Who Started the American Revolution.* Simon & Schuster, 1988.

McCullough, David. *John Adams.* Simon & Schuster, 2001.

McDougall, Walter A. *Freedom Just Around the Corner: A New American History, 1585–1828.* Harper Collins. 2004.

Middlekauff, Robert. *The Glorious Cause.* Oxford University Press, 1982.

Miller, John C. *Origins of the American Revolution.* Little Brown, 1943.

Wood, Gordon S. *Empire of Liberty A History of the Early Republic, 1789–1815 (Oxford History of the United States).* Oxford University Press, 2009.

INDEX

Adams, John, 9, 13, 34
American Independence, 9, 41
American Loyalists
    rights of, 9
Annapolis Convention, 14
Anti-Federalist Papers, 29
Appalachian Mountains (U.S.), 11
Articles of Confederation, 8, 10, 13,
    14, 16, 18, 27
    ratification, 10

Bank of the United States, 39
Bill of Rights (U.S.), 30-33
Bowdoin, Governor James (Mass.),
    15
British defeat, 8

Caribbean, 9
central government, 10-11, 13–14,
    17, 19, 21, 27, 29
colonial debts, 9
commerce, 14, 19, 22
Confederation Congress, 11, 13
Connecticut Compromise, 20–21
Constitution (U.S.), 5, 10, 16-19,
    22–24, 30–33, 39-40
amendments, 11, 31, 30–33. *See* Bill
    of Rights (U.S.).
    Preamble, 23
    ratification, 26, 27
    Virginia delegation, 16
Constitutional Convention, 4–5,
    16–19, 24, 26–27, 34
Continental Army, 4, 8, 16
Continental Congress, 10, 30
Cornwallis, Lord Charles (Britain), 8
Court System, 11, 22, 36

debt at par, 38
Declaration of Independence (1776),
    10, 30, 40
Declaration of Rights (Va.), 31

delegates, 5, 14r, 17–19, 21, 22, 24,
    26
Dickinson, John, 18
duties on intrastate goods, 13

Electoral College, 22, 24, 34
excise tax, 38
Federalist Papers, 27–29
France, 8, 9
Franklin, Benjamin, 5, 9, 17, 24
French Revolution, 40

government (US)
    executive branch, 18, 22, 35
    judicial branch, 18, 22
    legislative branch, 18, 22
    checks and balances, 22, 24
    separation of power, 22
Great Britain, 8–9, 10, 11
Great Compromise, 16, 20, 21
    voting on, 21

Hamilton, Alexander, 14, 20, 22,
    26–28, 35, 37–39 and George
    Washington, 26
Hancock, John, 30
Henry, Patrick, 29
House of Representatives, 13,
    20, 22
    membership, 20

Irish Rebellion, 40

Jay, John, 27
Jefferson, Thomas, 9, 35–37, 39
judges, impeachment of, 23
Judiciary Act, 34, 36

Knox, Henry, 35

land claims, 10-11
Land Ordinance, 11
Lexington and Concord, Battles of, 8

Louis XVI, King of France, 41

Madison, James, 14, 17,
    19-20, 26-28
Marshall, John, 25
Mexican War of Independence, 40
Mount Vernon (Va.), 4, 14, 34

New England, 13
New Jersey Plan, 19-20
Northwest Ordinance (1787), 13
O'Connor, Sandra Day (First US
    Women Justice), 36

Patterson, William, 19
Philadelphia, 16–17
Pickney, Charles, 13
Plantations
    cotton, 25
Potomac River, 14

republic, 10
Revolutionary War, American, 4, 6,
    8–9, 12, 14, 20, 22, 24, 28, 30,
    32, 36, 38

Senate (US), 20, 22–23
Senators, 22
Shays, Daniels, 14
Shays's Rebellion, 15
Sherman, Roger, 20
slavery, 13, 19, 24–25
    abolition, 24
Spain, 9
Supreme Court (US), 36

Thirteenth Amendment, 24
trade, American, 11
Treaty of Paris (1783), 4, 8, 9

United States
Constitution. See Constitution
(US).
territory, 9
government 18, 22, 24, 25, 35

Virginia (Va.), 4, 8, 11, 14,
16–17, 19
Virginia Dynasty, 36
Virginia Plan, 19

Washington, George, 4–5, 8–9, 13–
14, 16–18, 20–21, 26–27, 32,
35–37, 39
inauguration of, 34
oath of office, 35

Yorktown (Va.), British surrender
at, 4, 8